MW01534010

You My Hero

How to make your thinking and choices
determine your destiny.

Fast, Furious, Final

Dream to Direction

Read this and your life will never be the
same.

You My Hero   Uncle Wood

Library of Congress Cataloging-in-Publication Data

You My Hero/Uncle Wood
ISBN 978-0-9892560-4-9

Front and Back Cover Design by The Intelligent Consulting Design Team

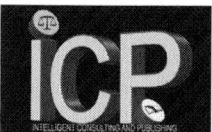

www.icandp.com

You My Hero   Uncle Wood

First give God the Glory, Honor, and
Praise for allowing me to be used by **HIM**

*This is a story of how a old man and
several teenagers turn hopelessness into
success.*

ACKNOWLEDGEMENTS

May I give a special thanks to all the influences and educators in the community and at the high school in BOONVILLE, CA. It is an honor to mention some of the educators. Though they were all great assets to learning, my relationship with some were very close so I acknowledge them here in a short but a meaningful thanks and honor. In no special order but here goes: JR, the Principal of the high school; a great gentleman, educator, powerful influence on the lives of the students, faculty and my close friend. Next is Tomlin, the Assistant Principal. His style of concern for the students and the faculty brought us together as men caring for the needs of the under privileged. Jeanie - a passionate teacher of American Sign Language, Spanish and mom to all. Next is Kathy one of the greatest math teachers on the planet with her kindness and aid to the students and to me. Then there's Page, a former co-worker at Lifeworks, math, gym, and coach. My hero Jill, a special resource teacher that taught me the special skill, of 'being patience, practicing patience, and allowing myself to be patience for the ones that have learning disabilities. Then Robert, Athletic Director, mechanics, construction and a go-to guy when I needed help during football and track seasons. Next is Julie, the history teacher who kept me up to date on all current affairs, both all over the world and here in America that I could pass on to the guys at Lifeworks. John co-worker at Lifeworks and coach at the high school, and Ms. Toohey can I say 'mommy bear'? Bill Coach, husband to Barbara, and ten plus years my Pastor at our neighbor church. And

You My Hero   Uncle Wood

to all the others that I failed to mention will
you forgive me? I honor you all.

Love Uncle Wood

_____

INTRODUCTION

Some scientists and educators believe here in the United States that by the time you are 5 or 6 years old, much of what you believe is learned about money, people, the world, what you deserve, what you can expect and how to (or not to) accomplish your goals. Funny, most of us don't know how to reach our goals or dreams because we don't have any. Also missing are positive role models that we can talk to. Can there be a solution? Yes! Where are our uncles? My name is Uncle Wood. In most books the introduction states in several pages why you write what you write. But with me, it's short, simple and straight to the x-rated stuff. Unfortunately each example given are brief stories of those involved but the principles are the real reason for the writing. Here goes...

This is a true story. The lives that are talked about in this book and the principles used are fact, not opinions. If practiced as a life style, then positive things WILL, and I emphasize WILL, happen for you. What do you do when hopelessness and hope collide? Listen closely to a solution. To wake up one morning homeless and without an income that's a hopeless situation. How I got there is a story of bad choices. How I got out came through some principles and a belief that there is a God. The application of the following principles can be seen in all the stories. First, get your spiritual life intact. Second, get healthy. Third, surround yourself with people smarter than you. I dare you to read this... it will change your life. The rest will be shown to you by reading through this book. Once again I dare you to read this... it will change your life.

There's more! One of the truths that came to me over the years was the need for role models in the lives of our families. Most of the teenagers throughout the States live in families missing Dads. There is a moral decay of our families. No more needed stats on fathers not being in the house or there for their kids. We can no longer hide the reality or fact that dads are **MIA** (missing in America). So my plea to the real Uncles is, teenagers are in desperate need of you. This is not to free dads partly or wholly from their post or duties, but Uncles can help fill the void of a male or males in their lives. This is my quest - Uncles with a plan to help teens to thrive and survive in this country. Some basic needs are shown in this book, but most of all is to show them Love .Hug them and listen to what they are saying. So as not to point fingers or the blame game, here's my solution to this dilemma; a reminder that hopelessness will cause change, for the good or bad.

Excuses we make to ourselves and to our kids:

1) I don't know what to do.
2) I don't have time.
3) I can't afford to.
4) I don't need to.
5) It's not my problem.

The list goes on. Stop it, Stop it, Stop it! No more excuses this is for real. The future of our country and kids depend on us. Uncles, step up to the plate. This book will show you how, why, when and where to help.

You My Hero   Uncle Wood

Remember the trials, tests and obstacles are an opportunity to succeed.

This is a story told and written by me in a form or style that would make my past English teachers cringe and question my mental faculties or the ability to spell, punctuate, form a complete sentence, etc. Now having said that, the names of individuals, companies, places and other identifying facts have been changed to protect the Identities of those mentioned in this story. Therefore any resemblance to actual individuals is merely coincidental (they know who they are).

PART 1 MY SPIRITUAL BOOT CAMP

When hopelessness comes in our life God is there too.

THESIS

A story of how an old man and several teenagers turn hopelessness into success.

This is a story about teenagers not knowing the love of GOD IN THIER LIVES and a born again, filled-with-the-spirit old man who God sent to love, respect and train them to be all they could be. Some did some didn't. Standing in front of twelve ethnic teenage boys who all had been released from the San Francisco Juvenile Detention Center into the custody of a group home facility (Lifeworks) located in Boonville, CA. They were sitting in a circle, one stood up with his muscular arms crossed in front of him and his head titled back slightly. His name was Logo; he was 18 years old, 200 lbs., buffed, chiseled and very muscular. He asked two questions, "Who are you and what are you doing here?" I said with a calm and authoritative voice, "I'm not your peer, your mama, your daddy, your dude, your homie, your nigga, your bitch, your probation officer, your welfare worker, your judge, or the police! I'm your 55 year old, black UNCLE WOOD. Call me anything else and you will piss me off and you don't want to piss me off. GOD sent me, now each one of you stand up and give me a hug."

"You my Hero"! This became my opening statement to all the young men I would soon meet (over 125 youth in ten years).

CHAPTER ONE

WHERE THE STORY BEGINS

The story of how I arrived at the group home (Lifeworks) in August of 2000, in Boonville, CA (will describe this place later) begins in my youth. I was born 9-7-1945, son of Woodrow and Frances Rushin in Akron, Ohio, and raised in an alcoholic environment with an extremely dysfunctional family. I was a very gifted child, let's say by the time I was in the 12th grade I had taken four years of A.P. English, Latin I and II, several forms of World History, U.S. History, Biology I and II, Physics I and II, Algebra I and II, Geometry Plane and Solid, Calculus I and II, and Trigonometry, but my greatest gift was relating to teen boys. I was caught in a time when in America hanging black boys was fashionable and the wars

You My Hero   Uncle Wood

(WW II, Korean and Vietnam wars) gave
some the chance to become second class and
middle class citizens, but amidst angry black
youth, KKK, Jim Crow whites, racism,
imperialism, greed, etc. I was asked to be
raised from a primitive state to a advanced
and relatively high level of cultural and
technological development based on the
knowledge shown at school! I was not bound
by the shackles on my hands and feet but the
slave mentality was present in my life. Yes, I
attended several of America's institutions of
higher learning both academic and penal. So
my life mirrored and understood the young
people I would meet in Boonville, CA.
Those who were marginalized, criminalized,
institutionalized, and without a true male role
model in their lives. Yes I understood their
home life and environment and why they
were considered throw-a-ways.

CHAPTER TWO

THE PROMISE TO GOD

It is said with genius comes success, but not always 'cause success designed by others is not what I was seeking. My dream was never considered by others, 'cause no one asked me. Let me pause and give credit to those who tried with all their heart to aid me on the decisions concerning my abilities and future, including one in particular, Herkie, my mentor. I heard him but refused to trust him totally. How could I, I thought that was my families duty. But my father and mother were absent in making choices in my young development; no family attachments, yet they were there in the house through all the years preceding their death, a home full of chaos ,daily, weekly, monthly, yearly. No family affection which led me to seek that void outside the realm of the home... much like the kids of today; parents letting the school and their child's peers run their lives, make decisions and/or influencing their lives; which brings me to the missed opportunities I had as a youth, young man and an adult. I made a lot of bad choices (I must remember that this is not about me but the God-experience I had prior to meeting the guys at the group home in CA, and the lives GOD touched there). The nights over the years living in my family's house were an endless weekend of alcohol, screaming, howling, fighting among mom and dad; me waking up with strangers on the floor, couch, or chairs who had passed out and didn't go to their homes. But this night was a lot different, guess I was about 10 or 11 years old. I watched as my dad took his shotgun, pointed at the head of my mother and told her, "I'm going to kill you this time #$$$%^&&." I was helpless, so I called on God and said to Him, "Please, please don't let my daddy kill my mother. I will do anything for You; I will serve You for the rest of my life." To this day I still get choked-up when I talk about it. I promised like a lot of us do when we need Him. God answered my prayer, I reneged on my promise.

CHAPTER THREE

THE YEARS FOLLOWING THE PROMISE

I soon got in the car with the devil. He took me farther then I wanted to go, kept me longer then I can remember, provided me with cars, lots of money, fine clothes, bling-bling, home paid for, ladies and more ladies ,drugs and more feel good substances. Then after many years of what appeared to be the good life, years of things that looked good, felt good and tasted good, things soon came tumbling down. I lost it all, everything; my health, family, friends and so-called friends. I was homeless. The devil left me to die with no hope, in the basement of a crack house, only place I had left to go. But that weekend when I thought I was going to die,

once again GOD showed up. This time, I
heard His voice. His words were clearer to
me than any voice I had ever heard. GOD
said, "It's not over yet, got work for you to do,
call your Auntie tell her you are coming
over." I did. I had meet Jesus, the journey
had begun. It is very difficult to describe a
GOD experience so I will do the best I can
and tell you about the results.

CHAPTER FOUR

AUNTIE AND THE CHURCH, PRIVATE TIME WITH GOD

Let me tell you about my Auntie, Samella Anderson. 90 years young, filled with the Holy Spirit, prayer warrior for Jesus. During the years of me being a servant of the devil, she prayed, begged, and cried that I would come to know Jesus. She greeted me at her door late that night and asked, "What's the matter?" I said, "Nothing, God sent me." She replied, "Well, God sent you, come on in take a shower and go to your room. It's been wanting on you for years." Auntie had a gorgeous home; I hadn't slept in a bed in a long time but hadn't had a lot of things in a long time that most people shared. Auntie never asked what had happened to me over the years. She would say, "Been a long time since we shared my home," and, "God will provide all your needs, let Him in your life," statements like that trying to assure me that God is God. He can do anything. By the way, the years had taken its toll on my life. 50 years old, weighed about 105 lbs., sores all over my face, dental problems, poor vision and in very poor health, no skills, no work history. Wow, a mess. I read this - 'Discouragement often comes when we feel like we've seen it all, heard it all, did it all and most of it was bad' (author unknown). GOD can do '...exceeding abundantly above all that you ask or think' (Ephesians 3:20).I had run away from God, but was given another chance to do God's purpose and will. I felt that I didn't deserve or qualify to serve because of past mistakes. But God chooses us based on grace; we can't earn a position to serve Him. Thank God for second chances.

You My Hero   Uncle Wood

Well this is how God took a mess and turned it into a message. Before I begin this testimony let me add something I learned during the next two and a half years. GOD will do several things but these three for sure (1) When, where or what arises, your provisions will be in place (2) The people God uses will surprise you (3) Your bad time is often when He does His greatest work. So here goes God's makeover .As I said earlier, I had nothing so I had to wash the clothes I had that night to have anything to put on the next day. That morning began the journey. God said, "Get up and walk around the block before you eat anything for breakfast." I started out the door and my Auntie said, "Where you going?" I replied, "God said walk around the block." Sounded easy, huh? Please, it took me a half-hour. I had to stop several times, this continued for a couple weeks until I finely could run around the block (your habits determine your future). During this time I had gotten saved and met a wonderful man, Pastor Samuel Hampton of the First Apostolic Faith Church . I'll never forget that day during afternoon prayer, which I attended Monday thru Friday for weeks. I walked in Pastor Hampton's office my third week in church. He said, "Can I help you?" I replied, "God sent me here to get you to baptize me, and you alone." He seemed unsure of what to do at that moment, but decided to assist me. I got baptized that Monday and joined the church that following Sunday. I must apologize for lack of details in my writing; the years gone by (age) have covered memories of the people, places, ideas, concepts and things. Therefore at times I will use statements or sayings that will provide you with the necessary clarity of the subject, now I shall continue. Using one of Bishop Hampton's gems, 'We are people who believe in God, Who is a Spirit, invisible, immaterial, and unknowable by any of the human senses. We believe that He exists and has control of everything spiritual and material. Because I believe in Him, I attribute actions, emotions and various phenomena to His functioning' (For nothing is impossible with God. Luke 1:37). Now having made it clear that I have, then and still do, faith in the Almighty God, the following events were amazing to see happen.

I began to obey God's every word that He gave me without question, which began to sound crazy to those around me. Let me interject a prayer that was similar to mine, very much like the situation I was in when people (new and old) were giving me conflicting opinions and advice. I was so afraid that I might make the wrong decision about my future. With this new way of life, my prayer was

Lord God, Your word says that You are the only wise God and I am desperately in need of You at this time. I'm in a situation human wisdom can't explain and human ability can't fix. There's only one way out-that's through You! Send the spirit of wisdom and show me which way to go. Send the spirit of revelation to help me understand what I can't figure out, for nobody but You can get me through this. Help me to faithfully obey all You show me to do, and to know the difference between human advice and YOUR Godly advice, and to choose Your way. I submit this situation to You and commit myself to following You, direct my steps, help me to walk this road with confidence in you with the courage that comes from knowing You, help me to cling to your convictions and to love those who do not know you and the ones that do ,take my hand Lord light my way keep me in your bosoms

You My Hero   Uncle Wood

for you know the end and all things will work together for my good and your glory in Jesus name amen (author unknown)".

CHAPTER FIVE

AKRON MACHINE INSTITUTION, DENTAL, THE FIRST JOB,

I was in enrolled in a trade school which seemed to me and others that this was impossible, let me elaborate. I was at the welfare office applying for foods stamps and my intake worker, whom I knew, informed me that to get any assistance I had to enroll in some type of training program. He suggested that I apply at the Akron Machine Institute. They were very good at training and excellent job placement. He didn't know I had no money, was not eligible for any type of grants or loans or that I owed outstanding money for student loans, but I gave them a call and made an appointment for the next open. It was two weeks away. I prayed to God he said

'Go.' By the way, it cost $2,700.00 to enroll. Unfortunately for me, my past gave doubt to all when I asked for money; sorry, no loans. I was a bad risk for any loans (including my pastor. Couldn't blame him) So when that day came I went down to the church and asked the pastor to give me a ride to the Akron Machine Institute, 5 miles outside the city of Akron. I told him, "God said it will be ok just drop me off." He asked whether I was sure. You'll never know what God will and can do for you until you find out He's all you've got. I was going on faith, arrived at the school and went to the window. The receptionist kindly asked, "Can I help you?" I said, "Yes, God sent me." She chuckled and asked if I had an appointment. I said yes, filled out the forms and took the entrance test. My score was second highest in the school's history. I noticed several people talking in the hallway about my test score, and then entered the financial supervisor. She asked me to follow her to her office. When I got to her office she told me that I qualified so how did I plan to pay. I said, "I have no money. God sent me." She looked puzzled and asked, "How about a bank loan, credit, grants, student loans, etc.?" I said, "None of the above, not a dime." She replied, "Mr. Rushin, with your score and since God sent you (with a smile), let me make a couple calls and see what I can do. Wait outside please?" A few minutes later she came out and said, "You can start school in two weeks, good luck." She shook my hand, smiled and went back in her office. I know now God had someone pay that tuition. On my way back home - a ten mile walk. By this time I could run two miles easily - I thanked God and thus reinforced my faith in Him. I had plenty of time to think over what just happened. My thoughts were to just tell everyone I got accepted. Forget the how, didn't need more about hearing from God in my life. Right then my relationship with most people was still fragile so hearing from God was questionable. My prior lifestyle of lying and cheating were still fresh in the minds of most. Well I started classes at A.M.I (Akron Machine Institute) in October, 1997. So there were several projects going on simultaneously while attending school. They were amazing... You be the judge. One of several amazing things began to happen. How would I get to class? Well the week began with me getting up at 4:00 a.m. reading two chapters of the bible, several scriptures in a little book (that I have keep and still read every day for 13 years), exercise (push- ups, knee bends, jumping jacks), then run at least a half mile (sometimes further) to a church, touch the door or go inside if open and pray, then back home, shower, and get dressed.

After all that then catch the 5:a.m. bus nearby to downtown Akron, catch another bus to school, I had to be there at before 7:00 a.m. So my school career began up at 4am, home at 5pm for about two weeks. When I met Tyre, who was attending AMI, he also was walking in faith. Tyre happened to live on the street directly behind my aunt's home where I lived. So here was my ride to and from school. Our friendship blossomed greatly to this day. We began to study the bible, class work, and even shared days of street ministry. Our time together developed into a true brotherly bond. I mentioned Tyre because he is a longtime friend who has been with me from the beginning of my faith walk and witnessed a lot of what happened. Like as I mentioned, I had a serious dental problem. God once again spoke and said, "Find a dentist, and go to him. Tell him I sent you." Being obedient I found the best in the area, made an appointment and went to see Dr. Raymand. Our first meeting went as follows: I arrived at his office (may I add, a state-of-the-art facility) and Dr. Raymand asked, "What can I do for you?" I replied, "God said you can give me my smile back." Well the problem was I had a serious dental mess. It would take several weeks to do, it would cost thousands of dollars, I had no dental insurance or money and I couldn't miss any more than one day of class per school policy. When Dr. Raymand heard all this, he was somewhat mystified. He pondered the situation then said, "Well if God sent you, I think I should make this a charity case and we will get it done." And he did 14 visits over a four month period and I didn't miss a day of school (got that beautiful smile to this day and haven't had a problem in over twelve years). My diet had also changed; fresh salads, veggies, turkey, fish, wheat bread, nuts, plenty of water, fruits, very little salt, sweets, no sodas, no fried foods, fasting and praying. There were times when alone with God, He speaks to your situation like this. Early one morning (4am) with about 3 inches of snow on the ground, before going to school I undertook my usual routine. I jogged to my church, went inside prayed, (seems like one of the sisters were always there) started back home and noticed there were only my footprints in the snow, the scene was cool, calm and beautiful but then I heard God say, "Those are not your footprints, I carried you." Wow, reminded me of the story called <u>Footprints in the Sand.</u> Moving on...

CHAPTER SIX

ME MEETING OLD MAN FRED (STUDENT) AND MIDDLE AGED ROBERT (CAD . TEACHER AT A.M.I.)....

These two became my closest friends at school; may I add they were both white, a relationship new to them and also to me. Let me expound on my relationship with Robert, the teacher in charge of me learning how to take a three dimensional object, apply trigonometry and the decimal system and draw it precisely on graph paper (different views top, side, bottom etc.), eventually on a computer. Robert had a terminal illness. He had heard about my faith in Jesus on healing and began listening to my story in exchange for a personal teaching during our lunch hour. His help aided me greatly, resulting in me graduating number one in my class .He attended my church several times to get to know my God, and Robert died a couple weeks before I graduated. I met his family and they thanked me for a being a friend during his final weeks. Fred was a retired sale rep who also, unbeknownst to me at the time, had a terminal illness (I found out a month after my graduation). He also heard about my walk with God, so he appreciated my company during our months together at school and at his home where we fellowshipped many times with his wonderful wife Marge prior to his death. I attended his funeral. May I say Fred gave me my first computer which aided me on practicing drawing on the computer using a CAD program that cost over $2,000.00 that Robert provided. I became very good at CAD. The story that astonished both Fred and Robert was my recovery from a former lifestyle, physical condition, being born again, and trust in God, which brings me to the day of the school's graduation party. I was presented with several awards; top student, perfect attendance, and highest scored percent in all classes. I was truly proud of myself. Later on that afternoon I was sitting in the placement office talking to one of the placement officers, Allen about jobs. The phone rang and he answered and I heard him say, "I have my top student sitting here in my office. I surely will." He turned to me and said, "Can you go to a job interview today at a manufacturing company in Cuyahoga Falls? They need a CAD operator right now." I did, and three days later I was working at Reuther Molding Co. Now here comes the faith part - I hadn't worked in fifteen years and now I had a high paying job. Wow! Tyre and I were so excited and we both remembered that Phil (his step-dad who worked at a car dealership) promised if I graduated and got a job he would provide me with a car. And he did, a really nice car. My skills at Reuther were truly appreciated because of my dedication, reliability and error-free drawings. Seven engineers who trusted my work; their jobs depended on my excellent work, thanks to God answering my daily prayers. My work ethics and skills got the attention of the owner, Carl Reuther, who called me in his office to congratulate me on my work, and to invite me to his church and tell how God had blessed me. He had heard my testimony from one of the guys in the engineering department. I did it; it was a pleasure to thank God and Mr. Reuther for the employment, at a Lutheran Church.

CHAPTER SEVEN

THE LAYOFF TO AKRON U, HERKIE AND THE CALL TO JACK

My time on the job was to be 3 months; it lasted for 7 months and then they sent me to Akron U. to further my CAD skills; a favor for the outstanding job while working at Reuther Molding Co. Then I was laid off. For the next two months I worked part time at the church. In the meantime, it was lots of reading God's word, watching and listening to Christian tapes and TV, (my favorite pastor was and still is TD Jakes) and sharing time with other Christians. Two I like to talk about briefly are Deacon Jones and Sis Bonnie (Bonnie and I were neighbors as children). We attended church together, they spoke in my life, encouraged and, prayed for and with me and provided me with their time and energy when and if I needed their help for anything during the whole time of my walk in faith while in Akron. So on a special day to me, Sis Bonnie called me on the phone and asked, "Can you come over my house? There's an old friend who would like to see you." I agreed. I arrived at her house a few minutes later and knocked on the door. She answered and asked me in. To my delight, there stood Herkie, my mentor. We embraced, it had been many years. The tears of joy flowed from my eyes. He too was delighted to see me. He was here from his home in South Africa. He had heard about my experience with God and wanted to see for himself. Herkie was astonished at the change so much he called an old friend of ours, Jack G., in Boonville, CA, and told him about my change. He handed me the phone. Jack and I reminisced for a few minutes and then he invited me to come to Boonville and work for him at his group home (Lifeworks) for at risk teen boys. I said, "Yes!" A couple weeks later I was in Boonville. Jack, Herkie and I were friends at Sacramento State University in California during the 70's (this was another God- arranged meeting). I must say a few more words about Bonnie and Herkie. They both have been true friends behind the scenes most of my life; may God bless them. Herkie truly believed that I had God-given talents, which even at 16 were amazing to this day. So that's my story and I'm sticking to it.

SUMMARY

1. Develop a relationship with God
2. Eat healthy and exercise
3. Surround yourself with smart people
4. Set goals and dreams on paper

5. Get a skill

Apply the above principles and enjoy the journey.

PART 2: THE BATTLE FIELD- MY
NEW ENVIRONMENT

Our life is not measured by longevity; our life is measured by the contributions and service we provide to others.

Jack picking me up at the airport and the two hour drive...

After a long flight from Ohio to California, I arrived at San Francisco International Airport. Jack was waiting for me at the passenger arrival gate. He was very cordial and smiled with a warm greeting. He recognized me. I, too, knew his face (strangely enough we both had aged 25 plus years). We grabbed my luggage, got in his car, and headed north for the two hour ride to Boonville. This was the time to get acquainted and to answer questions. The business questions came first, like did I get a copy of all my secondary transcripts (college and universities), criminal arrests and convictions, driver license, social security card, and fingerprint card. I answered, "Yes," to all of his questions. Then came the most important question of all. He stressed and asked, "Any alleged crimes, charges, or statements against you involving children?" I said, "No." Jack smiled and said, "You're hired. You got a lot to learn about these at-risk young men; these are the ones society and judges say are not fit to be among the law abiding citizens." This statement I had heard many times before. It saddened me for a minute, knowing my life also was tagged a throw away. But I shook off the feeling of sadness and asked, "Can we win this battle?" He said, "Yes. It's hard work, but we can win some... but we can't save them all. I wish we could." I replied, "I'm in." So Jack began walking me through the issues of the town of Boonville. Note: The 2000 United States Census reported that Boonville had a population of 820. The population density was 186.7 people per square mile. The racial makeup of Boonville was 703- White, 5-African American, 10- Native American, 4-Asian, 3 -Pacific Islander, 95-Hispanic or Latino. Jack was old school, so he called it like it was. Not the friendliest people in the world, but they respect each other. He told me what to expect from the people and our neighbors. That was all my whole body needed to hear, a safe environment. Jack talked about the scenery, school population, stores, source of income for most folks, the house, what was available to me; like vans, truck, and his car. First three months' rent free. Live-in residential child care worker - that was the job title. And the staff. Truth be told, the information was taken in but not a lot of thought was given to what was said. For weeks I had been praying for the right things to say to these teenagers. Pictures of hard core young men - drug dealers, carjackers, gang bangers, substance abusers, and the list goes on - flashed across my mind. In our society, a moral decay of our youth is taking place. We are losing our future, so there is a great need for people to know what is happening and how to do something about it. During this ride, memories from my past kept popping up in my head. Again the Voice spoke, "It's time for me to bury my past." So, hearing this, I said to Jack, "Excuse me while I bury my past and say an epitaph. My past ends right here, devil. Your hosts and your ghosts can't hurt me anymore. I'm moving on." Another thought that swirled through my brain was this fact. The guys in the group home had or would experience the feeling of fear that comes with the unknown or change... a new environment from the city to the country, for that was what lay ahead for me also.

_____

CHAPTER ONE

ARRIVAL IN BOONVILLE

Let me begin by describing the town that I would spend the next ten plus years in. Though Anderson Valley was a much different living experience for most of the group home youngsters, it was a safe, stable community where they could live as teenagers and do many of the things they missed doing in the cities. Nestled in the beautiful Anderson Valley were gorgeous mountain ranges surrounding a rural town with no malls, not even a stoplight. Expensive homes (which I would soon live in one) dotted the mountain sides which were filled with some of the most expensive grape vineyards and orchards in the country. I said with admiration, "This is God's playground.... a small country town with new people, places, things, and ideas held together by love and hard work."

CHAPTER TWO

DESCRIBE THE HOUSE AND NEW JOB

A ride that seemed to last for hours soon ended. We turned on a road that led to our driveway, which was a steep hill (300 meters long and used to train the guys). The house was gorgeous, made of all wood. It had three floors, five bedrooms, three baths, two decks that surrounded the first and second floors, two large dogs, a carport, a huge swimming pool and scenery that rivaled any landscape in the world - for real... my new home.

CHAPTER THREE

LIFEWORKS ACADEMY

Lifeworks Academy is a nonprofit group home that houses 10 to 12 teenagers in two separate locations. These juvenile delinquents (TERM USED BY SOCIETY) are ordered by the courts to complete at least 18 months in a Lifeworks program.

———————————————

CHAPTER FOUR

THE PUBLIC SCHOOL

Anderson Valley

Junior/Senior High School is a small rural 7th-12th grade school. AV high has 150 high school students and 75 junior high students. Several staff have experience working in county run licensed children's institutions as teachers or resident counselors. Most classes have 15-20 students and some of the advanced level courses have less than 10 students. This allows the teachers to give students extra attention and help. It is also so small that students can't hide. Students are expected to be in class and to participate. For many of the guys at Lifeworks this is a different standard. It's not enough to sit in class quietly and not cause problems; they need to produce work and participate. There was, of course, a learning period for these students where they had to un-learn the patterns they experienced in their city neighborhoods. Here they could relax and let down their guards and be kids. They gradually felt a sense of belonging in the school community.

Fortunately, AVHS and Lifeworks were on the same page regarding expectations. There was a built-in cooperative relationship. Lifeworks supported the academic program of the school with tutoring and homework support. For the first time in their lives many of these young men had a support system that allowed them to be successful in school. They also were able to share their experiences and opinions in classes, drawing from a life experience quite different from many of their classmates. Most boys were successful; however, the switch to a rural town and being away from their families, even if they were dysfunctional, was just too difficult for some kids. Also some boys were not willing to make the hard choices or able to follow the principles that would change their lives, but this story is about some of the ones whom did.

The group home provided the discipline and support so they received passing grades and improved skills, allowing them to earn honor roll status. Most of the Lifeworks students had never played organized sports even though some were very talented athletes. Anderson Valley often struggled in the numbers game for sports and with 10-12 boys; numbers could often make the difference in allowing us to field a football team. So Lifeworks students were a welcome addition to the athletic world. Lifeworks got involved in the sports program with their staff

You My Hero   Uncle Wood

(Jack was the head football coach for several seasons and I was the head track coach for eight years). All the athletes benefitted from their discipline, hard work and fitness programs. The Lifeworks guys played one or more sports each year; many of them played football, basketball, and track.

PART 3.: W.O.W

Having experienced a total makeover (spiritual, mental, emotional, physical and financial) at the age of fifty plus years old, using these knew found principles .Now being at lifework I felt this was God's way of providing the opportunity to help solve the problems plaguing our family (hopelessness) Here was the chance to see if this is an answer to the dilemma (what to tell our children). I practiced on teens in the group home and in the school that I would soon work in. I would motivate, encourage, and inspire young adults to succeed, using three words "YOU MY HERO" and some simple but powerful principles. It worked and there is a saying " facts are our friend". So I give to you my readers the facts. The guys are proof the principles work, you be the judge, also here was the chance to give adult role models a tool to use that help us bridge the gap between our children.

Throughout this section you will see W.O.W. WOW is a teachable moment that means' "words of wisdom".

CHAPTER ONE

LOGO

Wow. Most of what we want to do in life is hard. That's life. Encountering problems, discouragement and disappointment is inevitable. But we are destined to do great things. So any knowledge we receive about what makes us better at the things we want to do can be used not just to make us richer, but also to make us happier.

My first in counter with Logo was that day I arrived at the group home where I would live with the guys for the next ten years. My prior life style gave me an advantage over them because nothing they could say or do would shake my mission. The look in his eyes , stance, posture and tone in his voice lead me to discern this young man has seen some serious things in his young life; things that happened before he got to Lifeworks. Logo had many nights in the streets of San Francisco area where he was trained to be a street soldier for his crew, gang, set; the titles sometimes are confusing to outsiders but to me it meant his territory. 'Beware you enter at your own risk,' that was for all whom did not live there. Logo grew up with his mother Debby (who worked three jobs to support eight children), his father, Bobo, went to prison for homicide before Logo as born. Logo's life was like the scene in a real bad movie, where drugs, drives-bys, robberies and gangs were common. A 14-year old who smoked and drank. A young neighborhood terrorist making bad choices doing things I care not to describe for the sake of survival. A few years later his world came tumbling down; he was arrested and sentenced to six years in prison by a judge who stated Logo was 'a menace to society.'

Having reached that place of hopelessness
Logo said that prayer (most of us have said
this prayer also),"Lord please get me out of
this and I will never_____!" Three days
before he was to transfer to the California
Youth Authority his prayer was answered.
Jack G. offered Logo a chance to get out of
his mess and the surroundings. A deal to go
to Jack's group home instead of prison, a
eighteen month program monitored by the
court, a trip to Boonville, CA (Lifeworks), a
second chance, another way. Wow ... How
we respond to our life makes the results good
or bad based on our choices. Six months
later we meet. Logo asked, "Who are you
and what you doing here?" His story... Logo
was not an easy young man to get to know.
But what I did learn really fast, he was an
obvious leader. At my first meeting, I was
startled by his wrestler-like build. I guessed
he had been hitting the weights for some

time. His personal demeanor was that of a leader in the way he spoke and with the aura of confidence he projected. The principles covered in this book were being practiced in his life already. Case in point; number one he believed there is a God. In fact he was the leader of our church praise team every weekend at our neighborhood church. May I tell you that we, the young men at Lifeworks, helped build a new church in the town. Point number two, better health. By eating right, exercising, avoiding drugs and alcohol and getting proper rest; Wow! Knowing what to eat and exercise adds years to our lives. All the guys in the group home were on the high school football team. They won the championship the year I arrived, led by the team captain, none other than Logo. He led all the guys in the Lifeworks boot-camp-style workouts 5 days a week. Two hours a day of intense weight training sessions, agility drills, sprints and a 4-6 mile run. I joined them three times a week as I was in the program myself. It was a pleasure to have Logo's leadership along side of me while teaching the guys work ethics around the yard and in the community. And me being the new chief, my eat healthy formula... plenty of vegetables, fruits, nuts, wheat bread, salads, turkey, fish, pasta, brown rice, low sodium sauces, very little sugar and no candies. This was choice time for the guys to learn to eat right, but they had Logo to set the standard the rest followed the leader. Then our meals became habit, enjoyed by most of the guys. Remember, it's about the choices we make. Quick note, I had to learn really fast how to cook. Looking in the face of 12 hungry guys is frightening. Logo, having enrolled in high school, surrounded himself with smart people, some great educators and students, at Anderson Valley High School. Wow, critical thinking is hard work. That's why so few people engage in it. Logo became Class President, honor roll student, Homecoming King in his senior year, Captain of the football team, all league linebacker in his division and the first in his family to graduate from high school. After graduation the 5'9", 210 pound linebacker received a scholarship at the nearby Santa Rosa College and was also employed by Lifeworks. He set a goal to be the best at punishing running backs instead of rival gang members, and to get to a division 1 school. He had chosen to channel his prior violent behavior into a tough discipline routine that determined his destiny. He set goals that took a lot of discipline to achieve. During his first year at Santa Rosa College his football skills were noticed by Oregon State, Fresno State, California and others. But he had to stay another year because he had brought his younger brothers into the Lifeworks program and had to make sure they were secure before he could peruse his NFL dream. He was recruited on a full scholarship to Texas Christian University. The head coach at TCU once said, "I can't believe how short he was, but he was like a pit bull with a football helmet on. It didn't matter that he was small, because no one could block him." On his way to (maybe) a NFL career, tragedy struck. A leg injury interrupted his career. But in Logo's own words, "I dreamed of playing NFL football, but my goal is to get a degree." Logo's injury now fueled his goal with a passion to acquire a degree. So the next couple of years he would continue to pray, stay healthy and stay careful with the people in his life. His purpose, planning and refusal to stop produced a degree in Finance and in Sports Strength and Conditioning. After graduation from TCU he returned to

You My Hero   Uncle Wood

Lifeworks to give back some of his time and energy to help the guys at the group home. Now I had the privilege of working with Logo again for the next two years. In addition to numerous other feats, he is getting his Masters' in Finance, works out and runs 20 miles a day twice a week. He is my hero remember, it takes courage to succeed, for failure is common.

My name is Logo. To whom it may concern: I have had the privilege of working with Uncle Wood. His responsibilities included monitoring and maintaining safety of residents, addressing the behavior of residents with proper technique, conducting/monitoring resident academic plans, developing corrective action plans to address problems/issues, preparing meals, and training residents physically, mentally and emotionally to becoming productive members of today's society.

       Uncle Wood is a highly respected Residential Counselor, Mentor, Teacher, Coach, and Co-Worker for his willingness to assist anyone at any time. He has been instrumental in saving me from a ten year sentence in the penitentiary to a successful residential counselor, college graduate, college strength and conditioning coach, PE instructor, and father. Thank you for listening.

CHAPTER TWO

NOY.

In a room at the San Francisco Juvenile Hall sat Noy, an eleven year-old waiting on a judge to sentence him to a youth correction facility. He had been arrested again for selling crack and heroin in the Tenderloin, the drug jungle of San Francisco. At ten year-old he himself was using cocaine and smoking weed. Noy's father was dead and his older brother died in a stolen car accident. He was recruited to sell drugs by the older guys in the hood. He had quit elementary school, his reason being to help support his mom and seven brothers and sisters. May I add this startling note; his family was first-generation immigrant from Thailand. Hopelessness was surrounding a kid with no childhood or future. A great time to say a prayer, you think? So the weekend before sentencing Jack shows up with chance for Noy to make a choice that would change his life. He chose to go to Lifeworks, a group home in Boonville. So in 1995, Noy was a new resident of Lifeworks. A 4'11" fat kid with a nasty attitude was on his way to a new life.

I met Noy for the first time in the circle when I arrived my first year at Lifeworks in the year 2000 .I saw the potential in him in the months to come. Noy was every close to Logo, their bond was then and now very strong. Noy chose to follow and listen to everything Logo said and did to improve his life. This bond among Noy and Logo was unbreakable, then and now. I was extremely proud to be a part of these guys' development .Now back to Noy's story based on his input and my observations. He stated, in his words, "I didn't come from a world of easy living which included Little League, Boy Scouts, fun play grounds and street ball. Nope. Drive-by shootings, drug users, alcohol, drug dealers, pimps, hustlers male and female; no Disneyland, just chaos. That was my home before Lifeworks."

I had only to add encouragement with the love and patience of God into Noy's life. The encouragement that came from me was in the form of inspiration, strengthening and stretching his self-esteem. I spoke words like, 'You can do it, life is tough but don't quit, never. Noy, no excuses. Make adjustments.' He was very respectful of my instructions and knowledge. His devotion to staying in touch with his spirit, eating right, exercising, hard physical work, correct choices, positive thinking, studying to late hours into the night and being a servant to others. He made all of this a part of his life.

W.O.W. Opportunities to experience true success in life are blocked by excuses. His excuses were minimal. He made his days getting things done toward the future and keeping his promise to himself and others.

So 5 years later Noy had made great choices.

W.O.W. The ability to make a change depends on our personal thinking.

He was surrounded with smart people, tons of resources to learn from. Jack had supplied the group home with books, computers with internet, DVD's and a paid tutor. Now we had planned several goals to achieve and dream to fulfill. He had a dream to graduate from high school then on to college. He had now turned the fat into muscles and laziness into learning .Noy credits much of his success to discipline, the map to achieving goals and dreams.

His discipline was applied to the hard work in the classroom, and the sweat in the sports program at Anderson Valley High School. Through grueling workouts he became an all-league two-way line at 5'3" and 170 pounds (part of that team that won AV's football League Championship in the year 2000). Included in his success on the sports field at school was him graduating as an honor roll student (3.85 not bad for a dropout huh?) student body president senior year, leader in school and in the community. Another statement by Noy, "If you can put the same amount of extreme time and energy in physical conditioning, think what the results will be if channeled in academics. Your future belongs to oneself."

"My name is Noy. I was first introduced to Uncle Wood in August of 2000, while I was a resident of Lifeworks Academy in Boonville, CA. While I was there at Lifeworks, Uncle Wood became my mentor, my advocate and my trainer. Using some dynamic principles, Uncle Wood assisted in helping mold a petty dope dealer with no working skills, goals or ambitions into a family man and a positive member of today's society. Uncle Wood was my Math, Science and English tutor, my residential counselor, my track and football coach and eventually my co-worker. I was a Residential Counselor for Lifeworks Academy for nine years. I also work at Victor Treatment Center and have been working here for over five years. I also hold two degrees; one is a

You My Hero   Uncle Wood

Bachelor's of Science in Accounting from Sonoma State University and an Associates Arts degree in Liberal Arts and General Education from Santa Rosa Junior College. I am currently applying for colleges to get a masters degree in Business Management."

Hope this may encourage you to seek your future success using the example in Noy's experiences.

CHAPTER THREE

MARTIN

Sometimes a person enters into your life that you will never forget, for me it's Martin. Martin came into my life in the year of 2003. He had been brought to Lifeworks by his older brother, Logo. Martin's environment was identical to his older brother Logo, with a slight difference. Martin was a 12 year-old alcoholic weighing 280 lbs. A sixth grade dropout headed down the avenue of hopelessness, failure and death. But Logo asked Jack (head of the group home Lifeworks) could he bring his younger brother to Lifeworks before tragedy stuck his family again. A reminder, Martin's and Logo's dad was serving time in prison for murder, and mom working three jobs to support the other 8 children. Jack agreed to take Martin into the Lifeworks group. Now with Logo and Noy being his guide, these guys became the three musketeers.

At 280 lbs we all had work to do with him. He couldn't do one push up, run a hundred yards, and was much uncoordinated. Inspired by his brother Logo and Noy's success in sports and school, his passion was ignited. At this early age I and others saw that Martin was a very gifted child. So here was a great opportunity to nourish and encourage a youngster's desire to complete a dream. My role behind the scenes was to keep him in prayer, be his cheerleader, biggest fan, his coach (I coached at the high school) and monitor his daily activities. This was easy because he was very willing to listen. He trusted the elders and educators in his life.

Now at 15, he became addicted to learning and good health. He was making plans on paper. He had a glimpse of his end dream, with the persistence to get the job done. Logo and Noy kept him focused on the future. Sharing topics with him that most people never heard of like Sun Tzu, Machiavelli, Pluto, Socrates, schools of thought, the Art of War and TD Jakes. We were all careful with the people whom he associated with. One of his best friends was Devin (the son of the principal of Anderson Valley High School). They both had big dreams and enjoyed being around each other.

At this point in his life, Logo was off to TCU to pursue his dream, leaving Martin in good hands (Lifeworks, Noy and Uncle Wood). We were responsible to mold a kid into a productive young man. Martin had to develop character real fast. His future depended on him learning to trust others and adapt to his environment. He did an excellent job of following instructions without comment. This keeps him receiving knowledge and the passion for understanding. Martin's maturity grew at a rate that surprised us all. His intelligence increased with speed and determination. His physical stature was now beginning to sprout; he had a strong feeling of intense pleasure seeing himself as a supreme built athlete. But most of all he had great character, humility and a caring heart. Making the right choices became easy for him for he thought about most things before making a decision based on his knowledge and the advice of people smarter then him.

Now fast forwarding, he graduated from high school and got accepted at the nearby Santa Rosa Junior College, and worked at Lifeworks. I remember this day like it happened yesterday. Standing among members of our church, Martin asked for prayer for guidance, strength and courage to help him complete a dream to play NFL football. It was the year 2006; he was on his way to the Arizona State University. Things didn't work out at Arizona State U, so back to his neighbor. As time passed regardless of the situation, disappointments and difficult experiences Martin continued to mature mentally, spiritually, emotionally and physically. He constantly sought more information and how to use it to his advantage. His accomplishments began to add up and people noticed more and more of his potential. Once again he had to make a decision; continue on his dream or give up. His choice was to call an old friend, the defensive coordinator at Santa Rosa College. Time passed, things happened and he made the right choice Martin's most important football game of his life was Aug.21, 2011, as a defensive tackle for the New York Jets in the AFC Championship Game - Martin's first game as a NFL player.

W.O.W. Our destiny is not measured by the things we encounter; it is measured by the choices we make.

My name is Martin and I am writing this letter on Woodrow Rushin's (Uncle Wood) behalf. I have known Uncle Wood for ten years while I lived at Life Works and attended high school at Anderson Valley Junior/Senior High in Boonville, CA. He was a great mentor for me while I lived there. He helped me acclimate myself to my new environment, which was not easy as I had just left home from a city to small-town Boonville. Uncle Wood helped me through some hard times and taught me a lot in my years at Life Works. He was always approachable and willing to help in whatever way he could.

Uncle Wood was not only a mentor to me, but to all of us who lived at Life Works and the whole Anderson Valley community. He was the Head Coach of the Anderson Valley track team for many years and was a coach on the football team as well. He not only coached, but filmed all the football games too. He never missed a game or practice and was always prepared. He was very committed to his teams as well as his job at Life Works. Uncle Wood is very reliable and always found ways to connect with the youth. He is excellent at mentoring youth and this showed in the relationships that he maintained with his athletes and Life Works residents.

Uncle Wood and I have maintained communication throughout the years. Even though I currently am employed by the NFL and made it far in my football career, I will never forget everything that Uncle Wood did for me. How he mentored me and filmed my football games so that I would have film to give to colleges. I strongly believe that I would not have made this far in my career without Uncle Wood's counseling and support. He not only helped me prepare myself physically for the life I had ahead of me, but most importantly he helped prepare me spiritually, mentally and emotionally. He taught me life-long lessons that have allowed me to advance in my life. Thank you for your time.

W.O.W. dreams driven by decisions and passion produce results a stumble is not failure.

CHAPTER FOUR

JAIME

Jaime DeVicarra at 12 years old, let us begin. Jaime lived in a one bedroom apartment in the Mission District of San Francisco (the hood). His mom was 28 years old and from South America. Mom was unemployed, spoke no English and was very abusive physically and mentally to Jaime. He never knew his father. Also living in the house was his 35 year old cousin (from somewhere in Central America). Jaime's bedroom, bathroom and playroom were a closet. Their daily fight for food and money was begging, stealing, and/or odd jobs. In addition to all those problems, Jaime had anger issues, a weed habit and gang relations. This lifestyle continued for Jaime over the next few years. He had several arrests during this time in his life. Soon the city of San Francisco tagged Jaime as a menace to society. After, again, an arrest for stealing the Judge was furious. Jaime was waiting to be sentenced to the juvenile youth facility. He was struggling emotionally, physically and spiritually. Hopelessness had shown its ugly face.

W.O.W. We must hold on to the faith there is a God and He is able to change our circumstances.

Jaime prayed for help. Jack, the director of Lifeworks, intervened on Jaime's behalf. The judge had a sudden change of heart. He sentenced Jaime to 18 months at the group home Lifeworks. Jaime had spent 5 months in custody.

Jaime arrived at Lifeworks on August 1, 2003, he was 14. The day I met him I gave him my opening speech. When I asked for a hug, he embraced me with a long warm hug. The stone cold facial expression disappeared and a smile shone on his face. Later I would find out this was his first hug or sign of affection from an adult male that he could remember. I was his new uncle. This was the beginning of our bonding. His trust in me grew stronger as the weeks passed. I soon discovered he enjoyed talking and being around me.

Every youth that came to Lifeworks from juvenile hall corrections came with a file. This file contained confidential information. But I can say his school records showed that he had a GPA of 0.450. Also, his medical records stated he had ADHD.

You My Hero   Uncle Wood

.W.O.W Life can put you where you and only you can make the right choices.

After his third week at Lifeworks I asked him, "Are you ready to begin a journey to success?" His reply was, "Why not?" The beginning is the beginning, prayer helps in all matter. By now, I had been training the guys in the house (**LIFEWORKS**) for a few years. The principles of success were presented to Jamie. I began by telling Jaime, "I have discovered through trial and error, these principles for success.

GET YOUR spiritual life in tune with God. You must eat right and exercise. Jamie, surround yourself with people smarter than you. You must set goals on paper that others can see and monitor. You will need to build character and a skill. You must stay in a safe environment   while   developing   these principles. Last of all make the choices that will help push you to your destiny. In addition trust that God will help you to your future He's got your back."

Starting with his prayer life for he told me he did pray. Nice start there. His health was a daily challenge. His body was under developed. So the right food, physical workout and outside work became his routine. He learned quickly that hard work was not punishment. But it was part of a process of development. He began to mature physically. His mental state, getting over the home abuse was slow. But one of the fascinating things about him was how he handled his ADHD .He learned to focus on only one thing for a given time then move to the next. What came with the ADHD was his ability to remember 90% of what he read or heard. Think about the ways to use this talent

.What he did when school began amazed all around him. The teachers were delighted to have him in class. He loved learning.

The world offers many pursuits that cater to our desires— power, love, security, wealth, friends, health, popularity, prominence, prestige, and the list goes on. But in my observation, knowledge is available to all that seek it. This coupled with understanding gives those who obtain it a sure advantage to achieve their dreams, desires and success. I encouraged Jaime to pursue knowledge and understanding. He did, at an astonishing rate that surprised all those around him. Let me explain. The house had a huge array of books available to the residents. Jaime began to read book after book, while asking me could I get him special chosen books that he had found online. I said, "Of course." He had a goal of graduating from high school top of his class (he did). He reminded me of myself, many years ago. Jaime's quote found in the yearbook (2007) as a senior, 'The more you know about how to make your ambitions real, the closer you are to fulfilling them. It's up to you to make it happen.'

Jaime made me so proud of the choices he made. Take for instance, as a junior he applied for a summer internship at Sanford University. The program required that the student have a 3.75 GPA (by now Jaime had a 3.90). Additionally, the other requirement was a letter of recommendation from the high school. He had Jack (director of Lifeworks) and several teachers and others write him outstanding letters, along with his own written plea for the position. He was granted a summer internship at Stanford University.

W.O.W .the right choices may require you to leave your comfort zone.

HE took the risk that comes with change and success at Sanford and opened the doors to scholarships after graduation.

Jaime's development in sports was limited during his time in high school. One year he broke his arm while training for the track team (playing around). During a successful football season he broke his collar bone.

W.O.W. Interruptions' sometimes change our destiny.

So this left him with time to study while the rest of the guys played sports.

You My Hero   Uncle Wood

As the years of studying, planning and making the right decisions, to accomplish goals went by, Jaime graduated from Anderson Valley High School with a 4.2 GPA and scholarships monies from several sources, and most of all a partial scholarship to one of California's top universities - Davis University. The tears of joy streamed down my face. I was so proud of his accomplishments.

CHAPTER FIVE

JESSY

Graduate 6/6/2010

Jessy came to Lifeworks on December 30, 2006. Let me rephrase that statement. Jessy's dad brought him to Lifeworks in a desperate and hopelessness situation. Jessy was a product of a single parent (his dad) who was never around. This left Jessy home for several years without structure, discipline and direction. He made the choices which led him to drugs early in his life. Now with him and his dad in hopelessness, his dad prayed for help. So he brought him to Lifeworks with hope that Jack would let him stay. Jack said yes. They would work out the money details. Jessy's dad was upper middle class.

Jessy was a very pale white kid, 110 lbs., weakling, a serious acne problem, poor grades, low self-esteem, a health mess, and, let me add, had a weed and meth drug habit.

W.O.W time to meet God on his terms,.

By now I had been here at Lifeworks going on six years. What was an experiment with a system of principles to succeed now was a program that has prior success. In addition to Jessy's opportunity to change, this was a perfect chance to try all the principles. Jessy looked at his situation. With help from the guys he would start with his health. So Jessy had to pay attention, but he was a walking corpse. The guys named him Powder because he had the color of a corpse. By the way, he lived at Jack's house. Jessy was not a ward of the court but a favor from Jack to Jessy's dad.

All the guys did everything together like eating, working out, playing, school, studying, sports, entertainment, and growing. So I had the opportunity to help Jessy in all areas of his life. At the time Jessy arrived I was the track coach at the high school .I was an Elder in the church, the cook, van driver, tutor, mentor, and most of all, Uncle Wood. We attached immediately. He trusted what I said, but questioned everything. The questioning was alright with me. In addition to him trusting, he was humble (part fear), honest, and courageous to follow instructions without the comments of anger. Most of the guys didn't believe he would survive our rigorous training. But he was at different times under Logo's, or Noy's and/or Martin's personal tutoring, and guidance.

His short term goals were to get a 3.50 GPA his first year at AVHS, gain weight, get stronger, to be the fastest mile runner in the school, and read a book per month until he graduated. His long term goals - graduate from high school, go to college, get a degree in management, own a business, get married and have kids.

I was astonished at his development. We all followed a daily prayer that God help us to be kings, mentors, warriors and a hero to someone. Well all the guys were my hero. But Jessy took the decision to be my hero with passion and determination that I hadn't seen before. He was very smart in the choices he made daily in his life. I had to reinforce him time after time, that his future was his responsibility. He was the one who had the power and control over his future. Success comes by small deeds and actions done day by day. And he took the advice. Let me say right here I could not have asked for a student more willing than Jessy. There was one principle that he adopted with clarity. It was that being busy doesn't produce results. Productivity is determined by the right choices, extreme focus and action. Knowing now that his progress was awesome and remarkable, let me explain. He was getting stronger and gaining weight. He noticed this in the weight room. There was a wall mirror in the weight room. The guys could see their development. This visual gave the guys and especially Jessy, the motivation to put in the hard work to gain muscle. He wanted to be the strongest in the group home to assure guys would not make fun of his appearance and size. This visual worked so now my job was to encourage and document his progress. As time passed, Jessy grew bigger, faster and stronger at an astonishing rate. Jessy encountered the demons of failure, procrastination and distraction; He prevailed by making great choices.

Jessy's academics follow the same the path as his health and physical being. He was way behind in school (1.1 GPA) so I asked him to surround himself with the smartest guys in the house (Lifeworks) and at school. In the house, Logo, Noy and Martin were a great company of young men who had tried the principles and were successful. Also, they were staff at Lifeworks. These guys were outstanding students, so helping Jessy was their contribution to his learning. Jessy's avoidance of most teenage distractions and his desire and determination produced a 3.7 GPA. Jessy excelled in sports (football and track) and weight training (190 lbs. of pure muscles).On June 6, 2010, he graduated from high school with a 3.86 G.P.A. He accomplished several goals, short and long.

Having talked to him recently, he said, "I'm enrolled in my second year of college, playing football, 3.75 G.P.A. and working. Thanks Uncle Wood for your prayers, hugs and encouragement. Keep doing what you do, it works.'

CHAPTER SIX

XAVIER

Xavier brings to the table my hardest challenge. After my introduction speech, I will never forget his request. While embracing each other for several seconds of silence he said, "Please don't leave me, Uncle Wood." I was shocked. My reply was, "Never, I promise." Weeks later X (that's what everyone called him, X) told me why he wanted and needs my affection. His story was similar to this. I had to leave out the gorgy details. We meet Xavier (I will refer to him as X) in San Francisco, in a small apartment. Waking up to the pains of hunger was felt often. Missing meals was normal because mom (single parent) was an addict. There was very little money for food or clothing. Mom had not come out of her room in two days. So X knocked several times then entered her room to ask for money for food. She laid still in her bed .He called to her, no response, then he shook her, the touch was cold. X realized she was dead. He learned later she died of an overdose. The beginning of hopelessness surrounded X. He then went to stay with his Cuban-born dad who also was an addict. The physical and verbal abuse became a daily occurrence. Home was hell, so X went to the hood for food, peers and the need to belong to someone or something. The gang welcomed him and the cycle of crime began. After a few arrests and now sitting in juvenile hall not wanting to be there but hating home, X made that prayer 'God, please help me.'

W.O.W. Cries for help will be heard and sometimes are answered soon.

Jack came to the hall with a deal to come to Lifeworks, Xavier accepted in a hurry. The change in his life had now begun. One of the principles of success is changing your surroundings.

Once again, the chance to improve in X's life was based on his choices. He was enrolled in school. He made friends with most of the students, but he failed (in the beginning) at being a student. One of his challenges was he had a learning disability. His shame of this problem was covered up by making fun of other people. X was tagged the 'the sniper.' Let me explain. When people were having a conversation, X would butt in and say something to upset one or both of the people. Then he would laugh and walk away. This made most people upset and that was what he liked to do. This behavior continued for weeks. What made him like school was he was on the track team. He was an excellent runner. He had speed in the short distance and the ability to run for long distances. The school track team (of which I was the coach) was one of the best in the area. This gave X a sense of pride.

Now is where the success principles began. He had faith that his life would change for the better and God would help. He went to church with the other guys in Lifeworks and enjoyed going. Next was his health. I made sure he ate the right food. He began to treat every meal as his means of gaining weight. X weighted about 115 lbs, soaking wet. He had missed many meals but still was pretty healthy, just small in stature. His dream was to play pro baseball. This meant that he had to gain weight (long term goal).

So let's continue to follow him through the principles of success. One thing X had to learn and believe was that surrounding himself with smart people would help him accomplish goals, dreams in parts or whole. Having enrolled in school (10th grade) his classes were chosen by the school and him. He had a desire to be smarter than most thought he could be. Even though X was Special Education with a GPA of 1.84, he wanted regular classes. The good thing about this situation was that he was entitled to tutors supplied by the state.

W.OW God can provide all our needs

School would now be easier for him; there was help in school and in the house. By the way, Logo had returned from TCU to help run Lifeworks. Logo's return would aid X tremendously. Next, goals had to be made and priorities set by X starting now. Xavier made several short term goals, they were as follows: get a 3.00 **GPA** at school, read a whole book each month, get a California **ID**, open a bank account, get a social security card and a birth certificate. Long term: graduate from high school, go to college, play baseball at a college, and get a **BA** degree. I got to truly embrace his dream to play pro baseball because he talked about this for years. I watched guys in the house achieve their dreams many times. Now I had to also become his accountability coach. X needed constant encouragement. As we fast forward through the years at Lifeworks and in school, X embraced the new means to success; the principles set before him and now being used as tools for success.

School had soon become the means to help ensure his success. His mental state had now begun to flourish, along with a rise in his self-esteem. His involvement in sports (football, baseball and track), gave him great joy. His academics improved greatly, his GPA at graduation was 3.57. Life was going great for X. Graduation had come. He accomplished his short term goals. Some of X's long-term goals would soon be real. Discipline, determination and the right choices, had now appeared. The principles are as follows: spiritual, health, surrounding yourself with people smarter then you, set goals on paper and pursue them, gain a skill. X was now smiling at his life. The principles had become habit. X had become pretty much self-sufficient. As I write this part of his story. X is in his second year of college playing football, baseball and maintaining a 3.00 GPA. He calls me often to thank me for his success but I remind him I just gave him a plan, he did the work. He must thank God for the success.

PART 4: THE KEYS FOR EMPOWERMENT AND SUCCESS

1. LETS DEFINE THESE TERMS BELOW USED IN OUR LIVES AS SO WE CAN UNDERSTAND WHAT THEY MEAN SHORT AND SIMPLE IF POSSIBLE.

Prayer: the communication between you and GOD.

Faith: the power of God that available to you that can transform conditions, circumstances, and situations.

Divine Results: the tangibles, the things you can see, smell, touch or taste that are produced when you combine prayer and faith in God's will.

Goals: something that somebody wants to achieve.

Communication: the exchange of information between people by means of speaking, writing, or using a common system of signs or behavior.

Trust: responsibility for taking good care of somebody or something

Love: transitive verb to feel and show kindness and charity to somebody.

Concernment: a concern or matter of interest.

Intelligence: the ability to learn facts and skills and apply them, especially when this ability is highly developed.

Responsibility: authority to make decisions independently.

Honesty: the quality, condition, or characteristic of being fair, truthful, and morally upright.

Determination: the process of deciding on or establishing a course of action.

Confidence: self-assurance or a belief in your ability to succeed.

Workouts: a session of strenuous physical exercise or of practicing physical skills as a way of keeping in shape or as practice for a game or athletic competition.

Study halls: a period during the school day assigned for study rather than classroom instruction.

Work: details the physical or mental effort directed at doing or making something

Church: all the followers of a religion, especially the Christian religion, considered collectively.

Community Involvement: a group of people with a common background or with shared interests within society.

Accountability: responsible to somebody or for something.

Focus: concentrated effort or attention on a particular thing.

Performance: the act of carrying out or accomplishing something such as a task or action.

THE NEW MISSION

It has been my pleasure sharing these principles. We as adults now have words that can change the lives of our children. These principles work, now let us take them to our homes, neighborhoods and communities.

Let me give a reminder on what we have learned.

1. That prayer-the submission and dependence on God, seeking Him that He will do those things we cant and trusting in His ability to produce a desired result... Try Matt 6-33

2. Surrounding ourselves with educators, mentors professionals, and pastors whom can help with our goals and dreams.

3. Eating as healthy as we can and exercising, including physical work, or doing something three to five days a week that will keep us healthy for the rest of our lives.

4. Writing our goals and dreams on paper so others can read and maybe help.

5. People will pay you to solve problems so be good at something. Get a skill.

6. We are GOD'S servants, practice what you've learned and believe joy awaits you.

So here I am thousands of miles from California, in a new home and city with hundreds waiting on these principles. Then years in this city only God knows the outcome but what I do know is to give Him the Glory, Honor and Praise.

You My Hero Part Two Coming Soon

A SPECIAL THANKS TO

Dr. Vernon and "The Word Church" for your sermon "I'm Working on Something". You influenced me to finish this book. You are in my prayers.

Thanks to all that believed this would happen. God bless you all.

P.S. Tell the children The Principles and most of all reading you "You My Hero" will prove to you they work.

Made in the USA
Charleston, SC
13 October 2013